ALL-AUDIO
GERMAN
BASIC–INTERMEDIATE

ALL-AUDIO
GERMAN

BASIC–INTERMEDIATE

Peter Kellersmann

Based on *German All the Way*
By H. Singer and I. Lasting

LIVING LANGUAGE
A Random House Company

Published by Living Language, A Random House Company, New York, New York.
Living Language is a member of the Random House Information Group.

www.livinglanguage.com

Living Language and colophon are registered trademarks of Random House, Inc.

Designed by Sophie Chin

ISBN 0-609-81125-8 (cassette edition)
ISBN 0-609-81126-6 (compact disc edition)

Printed in the United States of America.

10 9 8 7 6 5 4 3

First Edition

ACKNOWLEDGMENTS

Thanks to the Living Language team:
Lisa Alpert, Elizabeth Bennett, Christopher Warnasch,
Zviezdana Verzich, Suzanne McQuade,
Helen Tang, Denise DeGennaro, Pat Ehresmann,
Linda Schmidt, Lisa Montebello, Marina Padakis,
• and Sophie Chin.

FREE ACCESS TO MORE
PRACTICE ONLINE

Would you like to enhance your All-Audio learning
with extra practice online? Go to
www.livinglanguage.com/bonus/allaudio/german
for bonus exercises, grammar review,
and culture notes!

How to Use this Course

This course was designed using an all-audio method that emphasizes spoken communication and, at the same time, gives you the flexibility of learning German wherever and whenever you'd like. However, if you prefer to see the course material written, we've also included this booklet for your benefit as a reference tool. After you have completed each lesson, you can go back and review the words you learned, or listen to the dialogue again with the text to help you recognize the spellings and constructions of specific words and sentences. Please note that this booklet is not a full or a direct transcript of the recordings: for example, the dialogue appears first in each lesson of the booklet, but will not be the first thing you hear on the recordings. We hope you enjoy learning German with our book-free, all-audio method, but hope that you will also take advantage of this booklet to help advance your German skills if you prefer to do so.

CONTENTS

DIALOGUES AND NEW VOCABULARY 1

Lesson 1: Greetings and Good-Byes 1

Lesson 2: Introductions 4

Lesson 3: A Telephone Call 6

Lesson 4: The Weather 10

Lesson 5: The Family 12

Lesson 6: In a Restaurant 14

Lesson 7: Grocery Shopping 16

Lesson 8: In a Hotel 18

Lesson 9: The Train Station 20

Lesson 10: Shopping for Gifts 22

Lesson 11: The Post Office 25

Lesson 12: At the Airport 27

Lesson 13: A Drive on the Highway 29

Lesson 14: Car Repair 32

Lesson 15: At the Doctor's 34

Lesson 16: At the North Sea 36

Lesson 17: The House 39

Lesson 18: Moving 41

Lesson 19: Sightseeing 43

Lesson 20: Exchange 45

Lesson 21: In a Café 47

Lesson 22: In the Mountains 49

Lesson 23: Sports 51

Lesson 24: Studies and Professions 53

Lesson 25: Daily Routine 55

Lesson 26: A Visit to the Dentist's 57

Lesson 27: At the Hairdresser's 59

Lesson 28: Pharmacies and Drugstores 61

Lesson 29: The Lost and Found 63

Lesson 30: Computers and the Internet 65

Lesson 31: At the Bank 67
Lesson 32: The Theater 69
Lesson 33: Festivals 71
Lesson 34: The Media 73
Lesson 35: Museums 75

GRAMMAR SUMMARY 77

The Definite Article .77
Der- words: *dieser, jener, welcher,*
    manche, solche 77
The Indefinite Article 77
Ein- words: *kein, mein, dein, sein, ihr,*
    unser, euer, ihr, Ihr . . . . Ihr
Masculine *n-* nouns 77
Preceded Adjectives 78
Unpreceded Adjectives 78
Personal Pronouns 78
Question Words 79
Forms of *wer* and *was* 79
The Demonstrative Pronoun *der* 79
Relative Pronouns 79
Reflexive Pronouns 80
Comparative and Superlative 80
Verbs in the Indicative 80

GLOSSARY OF GRAMMATICAL TERMS 82

ALL-AUDIO
GERMAN
BASIC–INTERMEDIATE

LESSON 1
BEGRÜßUNG UND VERABSCHIEDUNG
Greetings And Good-Byes

Im Büro

Herr Berger:	Guten Tag, Frau Steiner. Wie geht es Ihnen?
Frau Steiner:	Guten Tag, Herr Berger. Gut, Danke.
Herr Berger:	Und wie geht es Ihrer Tochter Monika?
Frau Steiner:	Sehr gut, Danke.
Herr Berger:	Wo ist sie?
Frau Steiner:	Sie ist jetzt in Berlin.
Herr Berger:	Auf Wiedersehen, Frau Steiner.
Frau Steiner:	Auf Wiedersehen, Herr Berger.

In the Office

Mr. Berger:	*Hello, Mrs. Steiner. How are you?*
M(r)s. Steiner:	*Hello, Mr. Berger. Fine, thank you.*
Mr. Berger:	*How is your daughter Monika?*
M(r)s. Steiner:	*Very well, thank you.*
Mr. Berger:	*Where is she?*
M(r)s. Steiner:	*She is in Berlin now.*
Mr. Berger:	*Goodbye, Mrs. Steiner.*
M(r)s. Steiner:	*Goodbye, Mr. Berger.*

Zwei Freunde in der Schule

Jörg:	Tag, Steffi. Wie geht's?
Steffi:	Ach Jörg, nicht so gut. Ich bin krank.
Jörg:	Das tut mir leid. Tschüß, Steffi. Bis Montag.

Two Friends at School

Jörg:	*Hello, Steffi. How are you?*
Steffi:	*Oh Jörg, not so great. I am sick.*
Jörg:	*I'm sorry. Bye, Steffi. See you Monday.*

NEW VOCABULARY*

Alles klar?	*Okay?*
Auf Wiedersehen!	*Good-bye!*
das Auto	*car*
die Autobahn	*highway*
der Bahnhof	*train station*
Bis morgen.	*See you tomorrow.*
Bis später.	*See you later.*
das Boot	*boat*
die Chemie	*chemistry*
Danke!	*Thank you!*
Das tut mir leid.	*I'm sorry about that.*
du	*you*
er	*he*
es	*it*
flexibel	*flexible*
die Frau	*woman; Mrs., Ms.*
gut	*good*
Gute Nacht!	*Good night!*
Guten Abend!	*Good evening!*
Guten Morgen!	*Good morning!*
Guten Tag!	*Good day!*
der Herr	*Mr.*
ich	*I*
ihr	*you (pl)*
die Intelligenz	*intelligence*
ist	*is*
ja	*yes*
das Jahr	*year*
das Kind	*child*
krank	*sick*
die Maschine	*machine*
die Medizin	*medicine*
der Mann	*man*
die Mutter	*mother*

* The abbreviations used in the new vocabulary lists are: *adv* for "adverb";
f for "feminine"; *fml* for "formal usage"; *infml.* for "informal"; *pl* for "plural."

2

nein	no
der Pfeffer	pepper
die Qualität	quality
schön	beautiful
die Schule	school
sehr	very
sein	to be
Sie	she; her; they; them
Sie	you (fml)
der Sohn	son
der Sommer	summer
die Sonne	sun
die Straße	street
der Tag	day
Tag!	Good day! (infml)
der Tisch	table
die Tochter	daughter
Tschüß!	Bye!
die Tür	door
typisch	typical
der Vater	father
das Vergnügen	pleasure
Wie geht es Ihnen?	How are you? (fml)
Wie geht's?	How are you doing? (infml)
wir	we
wo	where
die Zeit	time
das Zentrum	center

LESSON 2
VORSTELLUNGEN
Introductions

Auf einer Konferenz

Herr Breuning: Gestatten Sie. Ich heiße Fritz Breuning.
                Ich komme aus München.
Herr Wirkner: Freut mich. Mein Name is Eugen
                Wirkner. Ich wohne in Hamburg.
Herr Breuning: Angenehm, Herr Wirkner.

At a Conference

Mr. Breuning: *Allow me. My name is Fritz Breuning.
                  I'm from Munich.*
Mr. Wirkner: *Nice to meet you. My name is Eugen
                  Wirkner. I live in Hamburg.*
Mr. Breuning: *Pleased to meet you, Mr. Wirkner.*

An der Universität

Sabine: Tag, du bist Kirsten aus Schweden, nicht?
Kirsten: Nein, ich komme aus Kanada.
Sabine: Verzeihung.
Kirsten: Das macht nichts.
Sabine: Ich heiße Sabine.
Kirsten: Tag, Sabine.

At the University

Sabine: *Hi, you are Kirsten from Sweden, aren't you?*
Kirsten: *No, I'm from Canada.*
Sabine: *Excuse me.*
Kirsten: *Don't mention it.*
Sabine: *My name is Sabine.*
Kirsten: *Hi, Sabine.*

NEW VOCABULARY

acht	*eight*
Angenehm.	*Pleased to meet you.*
Ausgezeichnet!	*Excellent!*
Das macht nichts.	*It doesn't matter.*
Das stimmt.	*That's right.*
drei	*three*
eins	*one*
elf	*eleven*
Entschuldigung.	*Excuse me.*
Freut mich.	*Nice to meet you.*
fünf	*five*
Gestatten Sie.	*Allow me.*
haben	*to have*
heißen	*to be called/named*
Ich heiße . . .	*My name is . . .*
Ich komme aus . . .	*I'm from . . .*
das Jahr	*year*
Kein Problem.	*No problem.*
kommen	*to come*
Mein Name ist . . .	*My name is . . .*
neun	*nine*
sechs	*six*
sieben	*seven*
Verzeihung.	*I apologize.*
Viel Vergnügen.	*Enjoy yourself.*
Vielen Dank.	*Thanks a lot.*
vier	*four*
die Woche	*week*
wohnen	*to live, to reside*
zehn	*ten*
zwei	*two*
zwölf	*twelve*

LESSON 3
EIN TELEFONGESPRÄCH
A Telephone Call

Am Telefon

Sekretärin:	Hier ist Meyer und Ullmann.
Herr Kraft:	Meyer und Ullmann? Ist dort siebenundzwanzig dreiunddreißig fünfundfünfzig?
Sekretärin:	Nein, hier ist einundzwanzig dreiunddreißig fünfundfünfzig.
Herr Kraft:	Entschuldigen Sie. Falsch verbunden.

(Mr. Kraft calls again.)

Sekretärin 2:	Alfred Meyer, Frankfurt.
Herr Kraft:	Herr Meyer, bitte.
Sekretärin 2:	Wer ist am Apparat?
Herr Kraft:	Karl Kraft.
Sekretärin 2:	Moment, bitte. Die Leitung ist besetzt. Bitte bleiben Sie am Apparat.
Herr Kraft:	Aber das ist ein Ferngespräch. Dauert es lange?
Sekretärin 2:	Nein, ich verbinde jetzt.
Herr Kraft:	Danke sehr.

On the Telephone

Secretary:	This is Meyer and Ullmann.
Mr. Kraft:	Meyer and Ullmann? Is this twenty-seven thirty-three fifty-five?
Secretary:	No, this is twenty-one thirty-three fifty-five.
Mr. Kraft:	Excuse me. Wrong number.

(Mr. Kraft calls again.)

Secretary 2:	Alfred Meyer, Frankfurt.
Mr. Kraft:	Mr. Meyer, please.
Secretary 2:	Who is speaking?
Mr. Kraft:	Karl Kraft.
Secretary 2:	One moment, please. The line is busy. Please hold.

Mr. Kraft:	But this is a long distance call. Will it take long?
Secretary 2:	No, I'm connecting now.
Mr. Kraft:	Thank you very much.

NEW VOCABULARY

der Anschluss	connection
der April	April
Auf Wiederhören!	Good-bye! (on the phone)
der August	August
besetzt	busy
Bitte bleiben Sie am Apparat.	Please hold.
Dauert es lange?	Will it take long?
der Dezember	December
Dienstag	Tuesday
Donnerstag	Thursday
dreißig	thirty
dreiunddreißig	thirty-three
dreizehn	thirteen
Entschuldigen Sie.	Excuse me.
falsch verbunden	wrong connection
der Februar	February
das Ferngespräch	long-distance call
fliegen	fly
Freitag	Friday
fünfundfünfzig	fifty-five
fünfundvierzig	forty-five
fünfzehn	fifteen
fünfzig	fifty
Ich verbinde.	I'm connecting you.
der Januar	January
der Juli	July
der Juni	June
kommen	to come
die Leitung	line
der Mai	May
der März	March
Mittwoch	Wednesday
Moment, bitte.	One moment, please.
Montag	Monday
der November	November

der Oktober	*October*
das Ortsgespräch	*local call*
Samstag	*Saturday*
der September	*September*
siebzehn	*seventeen*
Sonntag	*Sunday*
verstehen	*to understand*
wählen	*to dial*
Wann?	*When?*
Was?	*What?*
Wer?	*Who?*
Wo?	*Where?*
Woher?	*From where?*
zurückrufen	*to call back*
zwanzig	*twenty*
zweiundzwanzig	*twenty-two*

LESSON 4
DAS WETTER
The Weather

Ein Wintermorgen

Frau Müller:	Guten Morgen, Frau Meier. Heute ist es aber furchtbar kalt und nebelig, nicht wahr?
Frau Meier:	Ja, das ist wahr. Gestern war es noch so schön.
Frau Müller:	Ich denke es schneit morgen. Was machen Sie denn diesen Winter?
Frau Meier:	Ich fliege nach Mallorca. Die Sonne scheint oft, und man friert nicht. Und was machen Sie?
Frau Müller:	Vielleicht gehe ich Skifahren.
Frau Meier:	Bis bald.
Frau Müller:	Auf Wiedersehen.

A Winter Morning

Mrs. Müller:	*Good morning, Mrs. Meier. Today it's terribly cold and foggy, isn't it?*
Mrs. Meier:	*Yes, that's true. Yesterday it was so nice.*
Mrs. Müller:	*I think it's going to snow tomorrow. What will you be doing this winter?*
Mrs. Meier:	*I fly to Mallorca. The sun shines often, and one doesn't freeze. And what are you going to do?*
Mrs. Müller:	*Perhaps I'll go skiing.*
Mrs. Meier:	*See you soon.*
Mrs. Müller:	*Good-bye.*

NEW VOCABULARY

auch	*also*
bald	*soon*
Bis bald.	*See you soon.*
der Blitz	*lightning*
Das ist wahr.	*That's true.*
Die Sonne scheint.	*The sun is shining.*
der Donner	*thunder*
ein	*a, an*
Frieren	*to freeze*
der Frühling	*spring*
furchtbar kalt	*terribly cold*
Gestern	*yesterday*
das Gewitter	*thunderstorm*
der Herbst	*fall*
Heute	*today*
kein	*no, not a*
leben	*to live*
machen	*to make, to do*
man	*one*
morgen	*tomorrow*
neblig	*foggy*
nicht	*not*
oft	*often*
schneien	*to snow*
schön	*beautiful*
schwül	*humid*
das Skifahren	*skiing*
vielleicht	*perhaps*
der Winter	*winter*

LESSON 5
DIE FAMILIE
The Family

Meine Familie

Freund:	Schau mal, Doris. Hier siehst du meine Eltern, meinen Bruder, meine Schwester, und meine Großmutter.
Doris:	Oh, das ist deine Mutter, nicht wahr?
Freund:	Ja, wen kennst du denn noch?
Doris:	Ich kenne den Mann da links. Das ist doch Max, nicht wahr?
Freund:	Ja, das stimmt.
Doris:	Deine Familie ist aber groß.

My Family

Friend:	*Look, Doris. Here you see my parents, my brother, my sister, and my grandmother.*
Doris:	*Oh, that's your mother, right?*
Friend:	*Yes, who else do you know?*
Doris:	*I know the man there on the left. That is Max, isn't it?*
Friend:	*Yes, that's right.*
Doris:	*Your family is quite large.*

NEW VOCABULARY

aber	*but*
alt	*old*
der Bruder	*brother*
dein	*your*
die Eltern	*parents*
euer	*your*
die Familie	*family*
das Foto	*photograph*
der Freund	*friend*
die Freundin	*female friend*
groß	*large, tall*
die Großeltern	*grandparents*
die Großmutter	*grandmother*
der Großvater	*grandfather*
die Hand	*hand*
die Hochzeit	*wedding*
ihr	*her, their*
kennen	*to know*
klein	*small, short*
die Kusine	*female cousin*
links	*left*
mein	*my*
die Mutter	*mother*
der Onkel	*uncle*
Ostern	*Easter*
rechts	*right*
Schau mal.	*Look here.*
die Schwester	*sister*
sehen	*to see*
sein	*his, its*
die Tante	*aunt*
unser	*our*
der Verwandte	*relative*
der Vetter	*male cousin*
Weihnachten	*Christmas*

LESSON 6
IM RESTAURANT
In a Restaurant

Abendessen im Restaurant

Bedienung:	Guten Tag, mein Herr. Was nehmen Sie?
Gast:	Ich nehme ein Wiener Schnitzel mit Reis und Bohnen.
Bedienung:	Tut mir leid, aber es gibt kein Wiener Schnitzel mehr. Essen Sie gern Fisch?
Gast:	Ist er frisch?
Bedienung:	Selbstverständlich.
Gast:	Gut. Dann geben Sie mir Fisch mit Kartoffeln und Salat.
Bedienung:	Was trinken Sie?
Gast:	Ein Bier, bitte.

Dinner in a Restaurant

Waitress:	Hello, Sir. What will you have?
Guest:	I'll have schnitzel with rice and beans.
Waitress:	I'm sorry, but there is no more schnitzel. Do you like to eat fish?
Guest:	Is it fresh?
Waitress:	Of course.
Guest:	Then give me fish with potatoes and salad.
Waitress:	What will you drink?
Guest:	A beer, please.

NEW VOCABULARY

das Bier	*beer*
die Bohnen	*beans*
bringen	*to bring*
empfehlen	*to recommend*
Es gibt . . .	*There is . . . /There are . . .*
essen	*to eat*
der Fisch	*fish*
frisch	*fresh*
geben	*to give*
gern	*gladly (adv)*
der Kaffee	*coffee*
die Karte	*menu*
die Kartoffel	*potato*
lernen	*to learn*
mit	*with*
mögen	*to like*
nehmen	*to take*
der Ober	*waiter*
die Rechnung	*bill*
der Reis	*rice*
das Restaurant	*restaurant*
der Salat	*salad*
Selbstverständlich.	*Of course.*
die Tasse	*cup*
die Torte	*cake*
trinken	*to drink*
das Trinkgeld	*tip*
tun	*to do*
zahlen	*to pay*
das Zimmer	*room*

LESSON 7
LEBENSMITTELEINKAUF
Grocery Shopping

Eine Einkaufsliste

Elke: Mein Freund besucht uns morgen. Unser Kühlschrank ist leer.

Anja: Ich mache eine Einkaufsliste.

Elke: Gut. Zum Frühstück brauchen wir Brötchen. Zum Mittagessen kochen wir Spargel mit Schinken.

Anja: Und ich backe einen Kuchen für deinen Freund.

Elke: Danke. Also, dann kaufen wir zwei Pfund Mehl, Zucker, und sechs Eier.

Anja: Und zum Abendessen?

Elke: Wie wär's mit zweihundert Gramm Aufschnitt und dreihundert Gramm Käse?

Anja: Gut. Was fehlt noch?

Elke: Zwei Liter Milch und fünf Flaschen Bier.

A Shopping List

Elke: *My friend is visiting tomorrow. Our refrigerator is empty.*

Anja: *I'll make a shopping list.*

Elke: *Good. For breakfast we need rolls. For lunch we'll cook asparagus with ham.*

Anja: *And I'll bake a cake for your friend.*

Elke: *Thanks. Well, then we'll buy two pounds of flour, sugar, and six eggs.*

Anja: *And for dinner?*

Elke: *How about two hundred grams of cold cuts and three hundred grams of cheese?*

Anja: *Good. What else do we need?*

Elke: *Two liters of milk and five bottles of beer.*

NEW VOCABULARY

das Abendessen	dinner
der Aufschnitt	cold cuts
backen	to bake
brauchen	to need
das Brötchen	roll
die Butter	butter
das Ei	egg
die Einkaufsliste	shopping list
fehlen	missing
die Flasche	bottle
das Frühstück	breakfast
für	for
der Käse	cheese
kaufen	to buy
kennen	to know
kochen	to cook
der Kuchen	cake
der Kühlschrank	refrigerator
leer	empty
die Marmelade	jam
das Mehl	flour
die Milch	milk
das Mittagessen	lunch
der Orangensaft	orange juice
der Pfeffer	pepper
das Pfund	pound
das Salz	salt
der Schinken	ham
der Spargel	asparagus
voll	full
Wie wär's mit . . . ?	How about . . . ?
der Zucker	sugar

LESSON 8
IM HOTEL
In a Hotel

Ankunft im Hotel

Empfangschefin:	Guten Abend, mein Herr. Sie wünschen?
Gast:	Ich brauche ein Einzelzimmer für eine Nacht.
Empfangschefin:	Haben Sie ein Reservierung?
Gast:	Leider nicht.
Empfangschefin:	Nur ein Doppelzimmer mit Bad ist noch frei.
Gast:	Was kostet das?
Empfangschefin:	Das macht 125 Euro, inklusive Frühstück.

Arrival at the Hotel

Reception Clerk:	*Good evening, sir. Can I help you?*
Guest:	*I need a single room for one night.*
Reception Clerk:	*Do you have a reservation?*
Guest:	*Unfortunately, no.*
Reception Clerk:	*Only a double room with bath is still available.*
Guest:	*How much is it?*
Reception Clerk:	*That will be 125 euros, breakfast included.*

NEW VOCABULARY

der Aufenthalt	*stay*
das Bad	*bathroom*
das Doppelzimmer	*double room*
das Einzelzimmer	*single room*
Es ist drei Uhr.	*It's three o'clock.*
fahren	*to drive*
der Fahrstuhl	*elevator*
für eine Nacht	*for one night*
gehen	*to go*
laufen	*to run*
die Reservierung	*reservation*
Sie wünschen?	*May I help you?*
die Treppe	*stairs*
Um wieviel Uhr?	*At what time?*
Was kostet das?	*How much is it?*
wecken	*to wake*
Wie spät?	*At what time?*
Wieviel Uhr ist es?	*What time is it?*
wünschen	*to wish*
der Zimmerschlüssel	*room key*

LESSON 9
DER BAHNHOF
The Train Station

Am Bahnhof

Beamte: Ja, bitte?

Reisender: Eine Fahrkarte nach Stuttgart, bitte.

Beamte: Hin und zurück?

Reisender: Einfach bitte. Zweiter Klasse.

Beamte: Wann möchten Sie in Stuttgart ankommen?

Reisender: Morgen früh gegen acht Uhr.

Beamte: Dann nehmen Sie den Inter-City. Er fährt um 23:30 Uhr ab und kommt um 7:45 Uhr in Stuttgart an.

Reisender: Vielen Dank.

At the Train Station

Clerk: *Yes, please?*

Passenger: *A ticket to Stuttgart, please.*

Clerk: *Round-trip?*

Passenger: *One-way please. Second class.*

Clerk: *When would you like to arrive in Stuttgart?*

Passenger: *Tomorrow morning around eight o'clock.*

Clerk: *Then take the Inter-city. It leaves at 11:30 pm and arrives at 7:45 am in Stuttgart.*

Passenger: *Thank you very much.*

NEW VOCABULARY

abfahren	*to leave*
ankommen	*to arrive*
aufmachen	*to open*
bekommen	*to receive, to get*
Bitte einsteigen.	*Please board the train.*
dürfen	*to be allowed to, may*
einfach	*one-way; simple*
erste Klasse	*first class*
die Fahrkarte	*ticket*
gegen	*against, about*
das Gleis	*track*
hin und zurück	*round-trip*
können	*to be able to*
machen	*to do, to make*
morgen früh	*tomorrow morning*
müssen	*must, to have to*
nach	*to*
die Rückfahrkarte	*return ticket*
sollen	*should*
spät	*late*
Türen schließen!	*Doors are closing!*
umsteigen	*to change trains*
wollen	*want*
zu spät	*too late*
der Zug	*train*
Der Zug fährt gleich ab!	*The train is leaving shortly!*
zweite Klasse	*second class*

LESSON 10
GESCHENKEINKAUF
Shopping for Gifts

Im Kaufhaus

Ulrike:	Seit zwei Stunden kaufen wir schon Geschenke ein. Ich werde müde.
Andrea:	Dann sehen wir mal unsere Einkäufe an. Den Regenmantel schenke ich meinem Bruder und die Bluse meiner Schwester.
Ulrike:	Und was schenkst du den Kindern?
Andrea:	Ihnen bringe ich die Handschuhe. Ich hoffe die Größe passt.
Ulrike:	Sag mal, wem willst du den Schal geben?
Andrea:	Meinem Freund.
Ulrike:	Oh, der Schal gefällt ihm bestimmt.

In the Department Store

Ulrike:	We've been shopping for presents for two hours. I'm getting tired.
Andrea:	Then let's look at our purchases. I'll give the raincoat to my brother and the blouse to my sister.
Ulrike:	And what will you give to the children?
Andrea:	I'll bring them gloves. I hope the size fits.
Ulrike:	Tell me, to whom will you give the scarf?
Andrea:	To my boyfriend.
Ulrike:	Oh, he'll like it for sure.

NEW VOCABULARY

ansehen	*to look at*
der Anzug	*suit*
bestimmt	*for sure*
billig	*cheap*
blau	*blue*
die Bluse	*blouse*
braun	*brown*
der Brief	*letter*
das Buch	*book*
Das gefällt mir.	*I like that.*
ein Paar Schuhe	*pair of shoes*
der Einkauf	*purchase*
dei Farbe	*color*
gefallen (+Dat.)	*to like*
gelb	*yellow*
das Glas	*glass*
grau	*gray*
die Größe	*size*
grün	*green*
das Hemd	*shirt*
die Handschuhe	*gloves*
hoffen	*to hope*
die Hose	*pants*
Ich suche . . .	*I'm looking for . . .*
Kann ich Ihnen helfen?	*May I help you?*
der Mantel	*coat*
müde	*tired*
Nein, danke.	*No, thank you.*
passen	*to fit, to suit*
preiswert	*inexpensive*
der Regenmantel	*raincoat*
rot	*red*
Sag mal . . .	*Tell me . . .*
der Schal	*scarf*
schenken	*to give as a present*
schon	*already*

schwarz	*black*
sich umsehen	*to look around*
die Straße	*street*
teuer	*expensive*
der Verkäufer	*salesperson*
die Verkäuferin	*salesperson*
weiß	*white*
zahlen	*pay*

LESSON 11
DIE POST
The Post Office

Auf der Post

Frau Klein:	Jetzt warten wir schon seit einer halben Stunde. Ich muss einen Eilbrief abschicken.
Frau Storm:	Und ich habe ein Einschreiben, deshalb kann ich nicht zum Briefkasten gehen.
Frau Klein:	Ah, Schalter fünf macht auf. Da kaufe ich auch zehn Briefmarken zu siebzig Cent.

At the Post Office

M(r)s. Klein:	*We've been waiting for half an hour now. I have to mail an express letter.*
M(r)s. Storm:	*And I have a registered letter, that's why I can't go to the mailbox.*
M(r)s. Klein:	*Ah, window five is opening up. Then I'll also buy ten seventy-cent stamps.*

Am Schalter

Kunde:	Ich möchte das Paket hier nach Kanada schicken.
Postbeamter:	Mit Luftpost?
Kunde:	Nein, Danke.
Postbeamter:	Füllen Sie bitte die Zollerklärung aus.

At the Window

Customer:	*I would like to send this package to Canada.*
Postal Clerk:	*By airmail?*
Customer:	*No, thank you.*
Postal Clerk:	*Please fill out the customs declaration.*

NEW VOCABULARY

das Abendessen	dinner
abschicken	to mail
der Absender	return address
die Adresse	address
alles	everything
aus	out of, from
ausfüllen	to fill out
außer	besides, except for
bei	at, with, near
der Briefkasten	mailbox
die Briefmarke	stamp
der Briefträger	mailman
dort	there
durch	through
der Eilbrief	express letter
das Einschreiben	registered letter
gehen	to go
die Idee	idea
die Luftpost	airmail
nach	to, after
ohne	without
das Paket	package
der Pfennig	penny
das Porto	postage
die Post	post office
die Postleitzahl	Zip code
der Schalter	counter
Schlange stehen	to wait in line
seit	since, for
die Stadt	city
dei Stunde	hour
von	from
warten	to wait
die Zollerklärung	customs declaration
zu	to, at, too

LESSON 12
AM FLUGHAFEN
At the Airport

Nach der Ankunft auf dem Flughafen

Anita: Dieser Flug war ruhig, aber der Rückflug kann stürmisch werden.

Georg: Hoffentlich laden sie unser Gepäck schnell aus.

Anita: Auf welchem Gepäckband kommen unsere Sachen?

Georg: Band drei. Die Tafel oben zeigt es an.

Anita: Wir müssen einen Gepäckwagen finden.

Georg: Dort drüben sind der Zoll und die Passkontrolle.

After Arriving at the Airport

Anita: *This flight was smooth, but the return flight might get rough.*

Georg: *I hope they'll unload our luggage quickly.*

Anita: *On which baggage carousel will our things arrive?*

Georg: *Carousel three. The board up there indicates it.*

Anita: *We have to find a baggage cart.*

Georg: *Over there are the customs and the passport control.*

NEW VOCABULARY

der Abflug	*departure*
die Ankunft	*arrival*
anzeigen	*to display*
der Aufruf	*announcement*
ausladen	*to unload*
das Bodenpersonal	*ground crew*
denn	*because*
dieser, -e, -es	*this*
fliegen	*to fly*
der Flug	*flight*
die Fluggesellschaft	*airline*
der Flughafen	*airport*
das Gepäck	*luggage*
der Gepäckwagen	*baggage cart*
hoffentlich	*hopefully*
hungrig	*hungry*
jeder, -e, -es	*every*
das Land	*country*
müde	*tired*
oben	*above, up*
oder	*or*
ruhig	*calm*
die Sachen	*things*
schlafen	*to sleep*
schnell	*fast*
sondern	*but*
stürmisch	*stormy*
die Tafel	*board*
welcher, -e, -es	*which*
werden	*to become*
der Zoll	*customs*
zollfrei	*duty-free*

LESSON 13
FAHRT AUF DER AUTOBAHN
A Drive on the Highway

Auf der Autobahn

Frau Lange:	Der Tacho zeigt schon 200 Kilometer. Warum rast du denn so?
Herr Lange:	Ich habe Hunger und möchte im erstsen Städtchen nach der Grenze Mittagessen. Da tanken wir auch und prüfen die Reifen.
Frau Lange:	Was? Du hast nicht genug Luft in den Reifen? Das ist doch gefährlich. Die nächste Raststätte ist nur 500 Meter von hier. Fahr doch dort hin. Da gibt's auch eine Tankstelle.
Herr Lange:	Ich kann doch nicht so schnell bremsen.

On the Highway

Mrs. Lange:	The speedometer shows 200 kilometers. Why are you going so fast?
Mr. Lange:	I'm hungry and would like to have lunch in the first small town after the border. There we'll also get gas and check the tires.
Mrs. Lange:	What's this? You don't have enough air in the tires? But that's dangerous. The next rest stop is only 500 meters from here. Why don't you go there? There is also a gas station.
Mr. Lange:	I can't brake so quickly.

NEW VOCABULARY

an	*at, on, to*
auf	*onto, on top of, on, at, to*
die Auffahrt	*highway entrance*
die Ausfahrt	*highway exit*
das Benzin	*gasoline*
bleiben	*to stay*
blinken	*to use the blinker*
bremsen	*to brake*
die Garage	*garage*
gefährlich	*dangerous*
genug	*enough*
die Geschwindigkeits- begrenzung	*speed limit*
die Grenze	*border*
hinter	*behind*
der Hunger	*hunger*
die Karte	*map*
in	*in, into, inside*
der Lastwagen	*truck*
legen	*to put*
liegen	*to lie, to rest*
die Luft	*air*
neben	*next to*
die Polizei	*police*
prüfen	*to check*
rasen	*to speed*
die Raststätte	*rest stop*
der Reifen	*tire*
der Sitz	*seat*
das Städtchen	*small city*
der Stau	*traffic jam*
stehen	*to stand*
stellen	*to put*
der Tacho	*speedometer*
tanken	*to get gas*
die Tankstelle	*gas station*

überholen	*to pass*
der Verkehr	*traffic*
vor	*in front of, before, ago*
wohin	*where to*
zeigen	*to show*

LESSON 14
DIE AUTOREPARATUR
Car Repair

In der Autoreparaturwekstatt

Herr Baum:	Können Sie heute noch meinen Wagen reparieren?
Mechanikerin:	Was ist denn nicht in Ordnung?
Herr Baum:	Er bleibt plötzlich stehen, dann springt er nicht mehr an.
Mechanikerin:	Gut. Ich überprüfen den Anlasser und ersetzte die Zündkerzen.
Herr Baum:	Und das Blinklicht rechts und die Hupe funktionieren nicht. Das Gaspedal klemmt manchmal.
Mechanikerin:	Um Himmels willen! Geben Sie mir den Zündschlüssel.
Herr Baum:	Er ist in der Zündung.
Mechanikerin:	Das Auto ist zwischen vier und fünf fertig.
Herr Baum:	Vielen Dank.

In the Car Repair Shop

Mr. Baum:	Can you repair my car today?
Mechanic:	What's wrong with it?
Mr. Baum:	It suddenly stalls, then it simply won't start again.
Mechanic:	Alright. I'll check the starter and replace the spark plugs.
Mr. Baum:	And the right turn signal and the horn don't work. The gas pedal jams sometimes.
Mechanic:	Good heavens! Give me the key.
Mr. Baum:	It's in the ignition.
Mechanic:	The car will be ready between four and five.
Mr. Baum:	Thank you very much.

NEW VOCABULARY

der Anlasser	starter
anspringen	to start (car)
der Auspuff	muffler
die Batterie	battery
das Blinklicht	turning signal
ersetzen	to replace
funktionieren	to work, to function
das Gaspedal	gas pedal
hängen	to hang
die Hupe	horn
in Ordnung	in order
Es klemmt.	It jams.
können	to be able
das Lenkrad	steering wheel
manchmal	sometimes
der Mechaniker	mechanic
die Mechanikerin	female mechanic
die Notrufsäule	emergency call box
das Öl	oil
plötzlich	suddenly
reparieren	to repair
das Rücklicht	taillight
das Schloss	lock
der Schrank	closet
stecken	to put, to stick
stehenbleiben	to come to a stop
über	above, over, about
überprüfen	to check
Um Himmels Willen!	Good heavens!
unter	under
das Vorderlicht	front light
wahrscheinlich	probably
die Zündkerze	spark plug
der Zündschlüssel	ignition key
die Zündung	ignition
zwischen	between

LESSON 15
BEIM ARZT
At the Doctor's

Im Wartezimmer

Frau Brink:	Warum sind Sie hier, Frau Kluge?
Frau Kluge:	Ach, mein Hals tut weh. Ich habe Kopfschmerzen und 39 Grad Fieber, und mir ist schwindlig.
Frau Brink:	Furchtbar. Sie haben sicherlich die Grippe.
Frau Kluge:	Und was fehlt Ihnen?
Frau Brink:	Ich huste immer in der Nacht, und die Hustentropfen helfen nicht.
Frau Kluge:	Das tut mir leid.
Frau Brink:	Ah, dort ist die Ärztin. Ich glaube Sie sind dran.

In the Waiting Room

Mrs. Brink:	Why are you here, Mrs. Kluge?
Mrs. Kluge:	Oh, my throat hurts. I have a headache and a fever of 102, and I'm dizzy.
Mrs. Brink:	Terrible. You must have the flu.
Mrs. Kluge:	And what's wrong with you?
Mrs. Brink:	I always cough during the night and the cough drops don't help.
Mrs. Kluge:	I'm sorry.
Mrs. Brink:	Ah, there is the doctor. I think it's your turn.

NEW VOCABULARY

der Arzt	male doctor
die Ärztin	female doctor
das Dach	roof
die Entzündung	infection
das Fieber	fever
glauben	to believe
die Grippe	the flu
der Hals	throat
halten	to hold
die Hilfe	help
husten	to cough
der Husten	cough
Hustentropfen (m pl)	cough drops
die Krankenversicherung	health insurance
Magenschmerzen (f pl)	stomachache
Ohrenschmerzen (f pl)	ear pain
der Schnupfen	stuffy nose
schwindlig	dizzy
sicherlich	certainly
statt	instead
der Traum	dream
trotz	in spite of
während	during
warum	why
wegen	because of
wessen	whose

LESSON 16
AN DER NORDSEE
At the North Sea

Am Strand

Tochter:	Es war toll im Meer. Aber jetzt habe ich Sand in den Haaren.
Mutter:	Trockne dich ab und zieh dich um. Beeil dich, sonst erkältest du dich bei dem Wind.
Tochter:	Das Badetuch ist sandig.
Mutter:	Dann zieh den Bademantel an.
Tochter:	Wo sind Papa und Jan?
Mutter:	Sie schauen sich Segelboote im Hafen an.

At the Beach

Daughter:	It was great in the ocean. But now I've got sand in my hair.
Mother:	Dry yourself and change. Hurry up, otherwise you'll catch a cold in this wind.
Daughter:	The beach towel is sandy.
Mother:	So put on your bathrobe.
Daughter:	Where are Daddy and Jan?
Mother:	They are looking at the sailboats in the harbor.

NEW VOCABULARY

anschauen	*to look at*
der Bademantel	*bathrobe*
das Badetuch	*bath towel*
sich beeilen	*to hurry up*
braun werden	*to get a suntan*
da	*since, because*
Das ist toll.	*That's terrific.*
Das macht Spaß.	*That's fun.*
dass	*that*
der Hafen	*harbor*
Leute	*people*
das Meer	*ocean*
ob	*if, whether*
der Sand	*sand*
das Schwimmen	*swimming*
das Segelboot	*sailboat*
das Segeln	*sailing*
sich	*oneself*
sich abtrocknen	*to dry oneself*
sich anziehen	*to dress*
sich ausruhen	*to relax, to unwind*
sich ausziehen	*to undress*
sich beeilen	*to hurry up*
sich erkälten	*to catch a cold*
sich kämmen	*to comb*
sich kaufen	*to buy for oneself*
sich setzen	*to seat oneself, to sit*
sich umziehen	*to change clothes*
sich vorstellen	*to introduce oneself, to imagine*
sich waschen	*to wash oneself*
das Sonnenbaden	*sunbathing*
der Sonnenbrand	*sunburn*
sonst	*otherwise, besides*
der Strandkorb	*beach chair*

37

der Urlaub	vacation
weil	because
die Welle	wave
wenn	when, if
der Wind	wind

LESSON 17
DAS HAUS
The House

Renovierungen

Ilse:	Gestern abend habe ich Wim und Maria besucht. Sie haben ihr ganzes Haus renoviert.
Sylvia:	Interessant. Haben sie alles selbst gemacht?
Ilse:	Nein, aber im Wohnzimmer, in den Schlafzimmern und Kinderzimmern haben sie die Wände selbst tapeziert. Und alle Fußböden, außer in der Küche und den Bädern, haben Parkett.
Sylvia:	Wie lange hat das alles gedauert?
Ilse:	Sie haben drei Monate daran gearbeitet.

Renovations

Ilse:	Last night I visited Wim and Maria. They've renovated their whole house.
Sylvia:	Interesting. Did they do everything themselves?
Ilse:	No, but in the living room, in the bedrooms, and the children's rooms they hung the wallpaper themselves. And all the floors except in the kitchen and the bathrooms have parquet.
Sylvia:	How long did this all take?
Ilse:	They worked three months on it.

NEW VOCABULARY

arbeiten	*to work*
das Badezimmer	*bathroom*
beantworten	*answer to*
benutzen	*to use*
besuchen	*to visit*
dauern	*to last, to take*
die Decke	*ceiling*
die Elektrizität	*electricity*
die Farbe	*paint*
das Fenster	*window*
der Fußboden	*floor*
der Hammer	*hammer*
interessant	*interesting*
das Kinderzimmer	*children's room*
die Küche	*kitchen*
der Monat	*month*
der Nagel	*nail*
nageln	*to nail*
das Parkett	*parquet*
regnen	*to rain*
renovieren	*to renovate*
sagen	*to say*
das Schlafzimmer	*bedroom*
die Schraube	*screw*
schreiben	*to write*
die Tapete	*wallpaper*
tapezieren	*to hang wallpaper*
verbrauchen	*to use up*
die Wand	*wall*
das Wohnzimmer	*living room*

LESSON 18
UMZUG
Moving

Endlich umgezogen

Arno: Wo warst du denn? Ich versuche seit Tagen, dich zu erreichen.

Knut: Ich bin umgezogen.

Arno: Hast du deine Möbel alle mitgenommen?

Knut: Nein, nur den Tisch, zwei Stühle, und die Bücherregale. Bett und Teppich habe ich zurückgelassen.

Arno: Hast du einen Spediteur genommen?

Knut: Nein, Peter ist mit seinem Anhänger gekommen.

Arno: Kannst du auch kochen in der Wohnung?

Knut: Ja. Ein neuer Herd und Kühlschrank sind in der Wohnung.

Arno: Prima. Wann kann ich zum Essen kommen?

Knut: Bald, wenn ich mich vom Umzug erholt habe.

Finally Moved

Arno: *Where have you been? I've been trying to reach you for days.*

Knut: *I've moved.*

Arno: *Did you take all your furniture with you?*

Knut: *No, only the table, two chairs, and the bookshelves. I left the bed and the rug behind.*

Arno: *Did you hire movers?*

Knut: *No. Peter came with his trailer.*

Arno: *Can you cook in that apartment, too?*

Knut: *Yes. There is a new stove and a refrigerator in the apartment.*

Arno: *Great. When can I come to dinner?*

Knut: *Soon, once I've recovered from moving.*

NEW VOCABULARY

anfangen	*to begin*
der Anhänger	*trailer*
das Bett	*bed*
das Bücherregal	*bookshelf*
das Erdgeschoss	*first floor*
erreichen	*to reach*
falsch	*wrong*
der Fehler	*mistake*
finden	*to find*
der Hausmeister	*superintendent*
der Herd	*stove*
die Hintertür	*back door*
Meine Güte!	*My goodness!*
mitnehmen	*to take with you*
die Möbel (pl)	*furniture*
richtig	*right*
sich erholen	*to recover*
die Spedition	*moving company*
der Spediteur	*mover*
der Stuhl	*chair*
der Teppich	*carpet*
umziehen	*to move*
der Umzug	*move*
versuchen	*to try*
die Wohnung	*apartment*
zu groß	*too big*
zum Glück	*luckily*
zumachen	*to close*
zurücklassen	*to leave behind*

LESSON 19
SEHENSWÜRDIGKEITEN
Sightseeing

In der Altstadt

Laura: Wie hübsch die Häuser sind. Und es ist so
angenehm, dass es keinen Verkehr gibt.

Olga: Hast du nicht gewusst, dass viele Stadtzentren
Fußgängerzonen sind?

Laura: Ach so. Hast du jetzt Lust den Marktplatz und
das Rathaus zu besichtigen?

Olga: Klar. Hast du den Reiseführer mitgebracht?

Laura: Wie dumm von mir, ihn nicht mitzubringen!

In the Old Town

Laura: How pretty the houses are. And it's so pleasant
that there's no traffic.

Olga: Didn't you know that many inner cities are
pedestrian zones?

Laura: Oh, I see. Do you feel like visiting the
marketplace and the town hall now?

Olga: Sure. Did you bring the travel guide?

Laura: How stupid of me not to bring it along!

NEW VOCABULARY

besichtigen	*to sightsee*
denken	*to think*
die Fußgängerzone	*pedestrian zone*
geradeaus	*straight ahead*
Hast du Lust?	*Do you feel up to it?*
hübsch	*pretty*
kennen	*to know*
die Kreuzung	*intersection*
langsam	*slow, slowly*
der Marktplatz	*marketplace*
der Platz	*square*
das Rathaus	*town hall*
der Reiseführer	*travel guide*
samstags	*on Saturdays*
tun	*to do*
überqueren	*to cross*
um zu	*in order to*
ungefähr	*approximately*
vormittags	*in the morning*
weit	*far*
wissen	*to know*
wöchentlich	*weekly*

LESSON 20
UMTAUSCH
Exchange

Umtausch eines Elektroartikels

Kundin:	Ich möchte einen Rasierapparat umtauschen.
Verkäufer:	Ist etwas damit nicht in Ordnung?
Kundin:	Er ist nur für 220 Volt. Ich will ihn aber auch für 110 Volt benutzen.
Verkäufer:	Wir haben keine Modelle mit Transformator vorrätig.
Kundin:	Dann gebe ich den Rasierappart zurück.
Verkäufer:	Ist er in der Originalverpackung?
Kundin:	Ja. Rechnung, Garantieschein, und Gebrauchsanweisung sind auch darin.

Exchanging an Electrical Appliance

Customer:	I would like to exchange an electric razor.
Salesman:	Is something wrong with it?
Customer:	It is only for 220 volts. But I want to use it for 110 volts also.
Salesman:	We have no models with a converter in stock.
Customer:	Then I'm returning the razor.
Salesman:	Is it in the original packing?
Customer:	Yes. The invoice, the warranty, and the user's manual are inside, too.

NEW VOCABULARY

der Adapter	*adapter*
benutzen	*to use*
Er funktioniert nicht.	*It doesn't work.*
etwas	*something*
der Fön	*hair dryer*
der Garantieschein	*warranty paper*
die Gebrauchsanweisung	*user's manual*
gegen	*against*
mit	*with*
das Modell	*model*
passen	*to fit*
der Rasierapparat	*electric razor*
die Rechnung	*invoice*
sprechen	*to speak*
der Stecker	*plug*
der Transformator	*converter*
umtauschen	*to exchange*
die Verpackung	*packaging*
vorrätig	*in stock*
zurückgeben	*to return*

LESSON 21
IM CAFÉ
In a Café

Ein Cafébesuch

Heike: Du hast wirklich ein nettes, gemütliches Café ausgesucht.

Sarah: Ja, schon als ich klein war, bin ich hierher gekommen.

Heike: Was soll ich denn bestellen?

Sarah: Probier die Sachertorte. Sie backen sie mit herrlicher bitterer Schokolade. Es gibt auch Joghurt Becher mit frischen Früchten. Dort drüben gibt's einen freien Tisch.

A Visit to a Café

Heike: You really picked a nice, cozy café.

Sarah: Yes, when I was a kid I always came here.

Heike: What should I order?

Sarah: Try the Sachertorte. They bake it with delicious dark chocolate. They have also yogurt cups with fresh fruit. Over there is a free table.

NEW VOCABULARY

der Apfelstrudel	*apple strudel*
aussuchen	*to pick out*
der Becher	*cup, mug*
bestellen	*to order*
das Brot	*bread*
drüben	*over there*
die Frucht	*fruit*
die Früchte (pl)	*fruit*
das Gebäck	*pastries*
gemütlich	*cozy*
der Himmel	*sky*
der Kaffee	*coffee*
das Kännchen	*pot*
köstlich	*tasty*
lecker	*delicious*
nett	*nice*
normal	*regular*
probieren	*to try*
die Sahne	*cream*
das Schlagobers	*cream (Austria)*
schlecht	*bad*
süß	*sweet*
der Tee	*tea*

LESSON 22
IM GEBIRGE
In the Mountains

Am Gipfel

Heiner: Die Sicht auf die Gletscher is fabelhaft. Besser denn je. Schade, dass wir absteigen müssen.

Volker: Die dunkle Wolke am Himmel ist bedrohlich. Und wenn es dunkel wird, müssen wir unten sein.

Heiner: Der Abstieg ist nicht so hart wie der Aufstieg. Geht aber über spitzere Steine.

Volker: Also los!

On the Summit

Heiner: The view of the glaciers is fabulous. Better than ever. Too bad we've got to descend.

Volker: The dark cloud in the sky is threatening. And when it gets dark we must be down.

Heiner: The descent is steep and goes over sharp rocks.

Volker: Let's go!

NEW VOCABULARY

absteigen	*to climb down*
der Abstieg	*descent*
Also los!	*Let's go!*
alt	*old*
atemberaubend	*breathtaking*
der Aufstieg	*ascent*
der Ausflug	*trip*
die Aussicht	*view, sight*
bedrohlich	*threatening*
beeindruckend	*impressive*
der Berg	*mountain*
der Bergsee	*mountain lake*
das Bergsteigen	*mountain climbing*
besser denn je	*better than ever*
dunkel	*dark*
fabelhaft	*fabulous*
der Gletscher	*glacier*
hinfahren	*to drive there*
hoch	*high*
mehr	*more*
der Naturschutz	*environmental protection*
der Pass	*mountain road*
schade	*too bad*
schnell	*fast*
die Sicht	*view*
die Spitze	*peak*
der Stein	*stone, rock*
das Tal	*valley*
unruhig	*nervous*
viel	*much*
das Wandern	*hiking*
die Wolke	*cloud*

LESSON 23
SPORT
Sports

Köning Fußball und andere Sportarten

Heinz:	Tor!
Eva:	Warum schreist du denn so laut?
Heinz:	Unsere Mannschaft hat gerade die beste in der Liga kurz vor der Halbzeit geschlagen. Unsere Stürmer sind am schnellsten gelaufen. Und der Torwart, Spitze!
Eva:	Schaust du die zweite Halbzeit an?
Heinz:	Natürlich.
Eva:	In zehn Minuten übertragen sie ein Tennis Match.
Heinz:	Tennis ist doch nicht so spannend wie Fußball.
Eva:	Sehe ich aber am liebsten.

King Soccer and Other Sports

Heinz:	*Goal!*
Eva:	*Why are you screaming so loudly?*
Heinz:	*Our team just beat the best team in the league, right before halftime. Our forwards ran fastest. And the goalie, first-rate.*
Eva:	*Are you going to watch the second half?*
Heinz:	*Of course.*
Eva:	*In ten minutes they're going to broadcast a live tennis match.*
Heinz:	*Tennis is really not as exciting as soccer.*
Eva:	*But I like it best.*

NEW VOCABULARY

bewundern	*to admire*
der Boxkampf	*boxing match*
die Fernbedienung	*remote control*
fernsehen	*to watch TV*
der Fitnessclub	*fitness club*
der Fußball	*soccer*
gesund	*healthy*
das Gewichtheben	*weightlifting*
die Halbzeit	*halftime*
heben	*to lift*
der Höhepunkt	*highlight*
Hör auf damit!	*Stop that!*
im Gegensatz	*on the contrary*
lang	*long*
das Laufen	*running*
der Leistungssport	*competitive sports*
die Mannschaft	*team*
natürlich	*naturally*
die Punktzahl	*score*
radfahren	*to ride a bike*
schreien	*to scream*
spannend	*exciting*
das Spiel	*game*
spielen	*to play*
der Sportverein	*sports club*
das Stadion	*stadium*
stark	*strong*
der Stürmer	*forward (soccer player)*
das Tor	*goal*
der Torwart	*goalkeeper*
die Weltmeisterschaft	*World Cup*

LESSON 24
STUDIUM UND BERUFE
Studies and Professions

Alte Freunde treffen sich

Axel: Lisa, seit zehn Jahren haben wir uns nicht gesehen.

Lisa: Ja, wir flirteten miteinander, machten das Abitur zusammen, feierten toll, und trennten uns.

Axel: Ich habe gehört, dass du Juristin geworden bist.

Lisa: Stimmt.

Axel: Alle Achtung! Hast du dein eigenes Büro?

Lisa: Nein, ich wollte in den Staatsdienst. Und wie ist es dir ergangen?

Axel: Ich bin Unternehmensberater geworden.

Old Friends Meet

Axel: *Lisa, it's been ten years since we saw each other.*

Lisa: *Yes, we used to flirt, graduated together from high school, celebrated wildly, and we separated.*

Axel: *I heard that you became a lawyer.*

Lisa: *That's right.*

Axel: *My respect to you! Do you have your own office?*

Lisa: *No, I wanted a government job. And what happened to you?*

Axel: *I became a company consultant.*

NEW VOCABULARY

Alle Achtung!	*My respect (to you)!*
der Architekt	*architect*
der Beruf	*occupation*
beruflich	*professionally*
die Bildung	*education*
das Büro	*office*
das Abitur machen	*to graduate from high school*
eigen	*own*
feiern	*to party*
Finanzen	*finances*
flirten	*to flirt*
froh	*glad*
der Jurist(in)	*lawyer (m/f)*
der Lehrer	*teacher*
der Maler	*painter*
miteinander	*with one another*
sagen	*to say*
die Schule	*school*
sich trennen	*to separate*
Spaß haben	*to have a good time*
der Staatsdienst	*government position*
der Unternehmensberater	*consultant*
Wie ist es dir ergangen?	*How have you been?*
zusammen	*together*

LESSON 25
TAGESROUTINE
Daily Routine

Ein schlechter Tag

Freund:	Tag, Jutta. Ich hab dich gestern angerufen, bekam aber keine Antwort.
Jutta:	Ich habe verschlafen und bin erst um neun aufgestanden.
Freund:	Hast du keinen Wecker?
Jutta:	Doch, aber er hat nicht geläutet.
Freund:	Wo warst du denn später?
Jutta:	Ich sollte um zehn zum Zahnarzt. Ich kam auch pünktlich an.
Freund:	Du bist schnell.
Jutta:	Hör erst mal wie es ausging. An der Tür vom Zahnarzt hing ein Schild: "Montags geschlossen."
Freund:	Was?
Jutta:	Und ich dachte es ist Dienstag.

A Bad Day

Friend:	Hello, Jutta. I called you yesterday, but didn't receive an answer.
Jutta:	I overslept and didn't get up until nine.
Friend:	Don't you have an alarm?
Jutta:	Yes, but it didn't ring.
Friend:	Where were you later?
Jutta:	I was supposed to go to the dentist at ten. I arrived on time, too.
Friend:	You're quick.
Jutta:	First hear how it ended. On the dentist's door was a sign: "Closed on Mondays."
Friend:	What?
Jutta:	And I thought it was Tuesday.

NEW VOCABULARY

die Antwort	answer
aufstehen	to get up
denken	to think
früh	early
gewöhnlich	usually
ins Bett gehen	to go to bed
läuten	to ring
lesen	to read
Montags geschlossen.	Closed on Mondays.
pünktlich	punctually
rennen	to run
das Schild	sign
schlafen	to sleep
später	later
unpünktlich	not punctual
die Verabredung	appointment
verschlafen	to oversleep
der Wecker	alarm clock
wissen	to know
der Zahnarzt	dentist
(zu) früh	(too) early
(zu) spät	(too) late

LESSON 26
DER ZAHNARZTBESUCH
A Visit to the Dentist's

Beim Zahnarzt

Zahnarzt:	Ihre Zähne sind gut. Kein Zahnbelag. Sie putzen Ihre Zähne sicher regelmäßig.
Patientin:	Immer!
Zahnarzt:	Zähne, die gut gepflegt werden, sind auch meistens gesund.
Patientin:	Aber der Schmerz, den ich habe, kommt doch von den Zähnen.
Zahnarzt:	Ah, Sie haben eine kleine Entzündung, die nur das Zahnfleisch betrifft. Die Wurzel, deren Röntgenbild ich gesehen habe, ist gesund.
Patientin:	Na, dann bin ich beruhigt.

At the Dentist's

Dentist:	Your teeth are fine. No plaque at all. You probably clean your teeth regularly.
Patient:	Always!
Dentist:	Teeth that are well taken care of are usually also healthy.
Patient:	But the pain that I have is coming from my teeth.
Dentist:	Ah, you have a small infection, which only affects the gums. The root, of which I've seen the X ray, is healthy.
Patient:	Well, then I'm relieved.

NEW VOCABULARY

der Backenzahn	*molar tooth*
beißen	*to bite*
beruhigt	*relieved*
Es tut weh.	*It hurts.*
immer	*always*
die Krone	*crown*
meistens	*most of the time*
der Notfall	*emergency*
der Patient(in)	*the patient (m/f)*
pflegen	*to maintain*
regelmäßig	*regularly*
das Röntgenbild	*X ray*
der Sessel	*seat*
der Schmerz	*pain*
das Schmerzmittel	*painkiller*
der Schrei	*scream*
der Termin	*appointment*
die Ursache	*cause*
die Wurzel	*root*
der Zahn	*tooth*
der Zahnbelag	*plaque*
Zähne putzen	*to brush teeth*
der Zahnersatz	*replacements*
das Zahnfleisch	*gums*

LESSON 27
IM FRISEURSALON
At the Hairdresser's

Im Herrensalon

Kunde: Waschen und schneiden, bitte! Aber nicht
zu kurz. Ich habe leider nicht mehr viele
Haare.

Friseuse: Wie wär's mit einem neuen
Haarwuchsmittel?

Kunde: Glauben Sie an Märchen?

At the Men's Hairdresser's

Customer: *Wash and cut, please! But not too short.
Unfortunately, I don't have too much hair
left.*

Hairdresser: *How about a new hair-growth product?*

Customer: *Do you believe such fairy tales?*

Im Damensalon

Kundin: Eine neue Dauerwelle, bitte.

Friseur: Soll ich auch färben?

Kundin: Nein, ich möchte wieder einmal meine
natürliche Haarfarbe sehen.

Friseur: Wann haben Sie mit dem Färben
angefangen?

Kundin: Als ich sechzehn war. Davor hatte ich
immer glatte, blonde Haare.

At the Women's Hairdresser's

Customer: *A new perm, please.*

Hairdresser: *Should I dye your hair, too?*

Customer: *No, I would like to see my natural hair
color again.*

Hairdresser: *When did you start dyeing your hair?*

Customer: *When I was sixteen. Before that, I always
had straight, blonde hair.*

NEW VOCABULARY

als	*when (past)*
der Conditioner	*conditioner*
die Dauerwelle	*perm*
färben	*to dye*
fönen	*to dry hair*
der Friseur	*hairdresser (m)*
die Friseuse	*hairdresser (f)*
glatt	*uncurled, straight*
das Haar	*hair*
die Haarfarbe	*hair color*
der Haarschnitt	*haircut*
das Haarwuchsmittel	*hair-growth product*
kurz	*short*
die Locke	*curl*
das Märchen	*fairy tale*
schneiden	*to cut*
das Shampoo	*shampoo*
wann	*when*
waschen	*to wash*
wenn	*whenever, if, when*

LESSON 28
APOTHEKEN UND DROGERIEN
Pharmacies and Drugstores

In der Apotheke

Kunde:	Ist das Rezept für Schmidt fertig?
Apothekerin:	Schmidt? Ja, aber wir mussten das eine Mittel bestellen.
Kunde:	Und wann werden Sie es bekommen?
Apothekerin:	Es wird sicher mit der Morgenlieferung eintreffen.
Kunde:	Und wie nimmt man die Tabletten ein?
Apothekerin:	Nach dem Abendessen, mit einem Glas Wasser. Es steht auf der Packung.

At the Pharmacy

Customer:	*Is the prescription for Schmidt ready?*
Pharmacist:	*Schmidt? Yes, but we had to order one item.*
Customer:	*When will you get it?*
Pharmacist:	*It will probably arrive with the morning delivery.*
Customer:	*And how should one take these pills?*
Pharmacist:	*After dinner, with a glass of water. It says it on the box.*

NEW VOCABULARY

die Apotheke	*pharmacy*
der Apotheker	*pharmacist (m)*
die Apothekerin	*pharmacist (f)*
die Drogerie	*drugstore*
eintreffen	*arrive*
das Glas Wasser	*glass of water*
holen	*to get*
der Kopfschmerz	*headache*
die Lieferung	*delivery*
das Mittel	*preparation*
möglich	*possible*
die Packung	*package*
das Rezept	*prescription*
rezeptfrei	*prescription-free (over-the-counter)*
rezeptpflichtige Medizin	*prescription medicine*
die Schlaftablette	*sleeping pill*
die Tablette	*tablet*
verschreiben	*to prescribe*

LESSON 29
DAS FUNDBÜRO
The Lost and Found

Auf dem Fundbüro

Touristin:	Ist hier eine Tasche abgegeben worden?
Beamter:	Bitte beschreiben Sie die Tasche.
Touristin:	Es ist eine braun Handtasche aus Leder.
Beamter:	Wann haben Sie die Handtasche verloren?
Touristin:	Heute nachmittag. Vielleicht ist sie gestohlen worden.
Beamter:	Beschreiben Sie den Inhalt der Tasche.
Touristin:	Eine Kreditkarte, eine Geldbörse mit Kleingeld, und mein Reisepass.
Beamter:	Es wurde keine braun Handtasche abgegeben. Aber vielleicht wird sie noch gefunden.

At the Lost and Found

Tourist:	Has a bag been handed in?
Clerk:	Please describe the bag.
Tourist:	It is a brown handbag made of leather.
Clerk:	When did you lose the handbag?
Tourist:	This afternoon. Perhaps it has been stolen.
Clerk:	Describe the contents of the bag.
Tourist:	A credit card, a purse with coins, and my passport.
Clerk:	No brown handbag has been handed in. But perhaps it will still be found.

NEW VOCABULARY

abgeben	to hand in
das amerikanische Konsulat	American consulate
aus Leder	made of leather
die Belohnung	reward
beschreiben	describe
die Brieftasche	wallet
der Dieb	thief
fangen	to catch
finden	to find
der Finder	finder
das Fundbüro	lost and found
die Geldbörse	purse
die Handtasche	handbag
der Inhalt	contents
das Kleingeld	change
das Notizbuch	notebook
die Polizeiwache	police station
der Reisepass	passport
der Schlüssel	key
stehlen	to steal
der Taschendieb	pickpocket
verlieren	to lose

LESSON 30
COMPUTER UND DAS INTERNET
Computers and the Internet

Ein neuer Computer

Andreas:	Und was kann man mit diesem Computer besser machen?
Gudrun:	Mit dem neuen Modem kann man schneller das Internet surfen. Und man kann Webseiten mit Grafiken oder Video herunterladen.
Andreas:	Lässt sich auch E-Mail schneller schicken?
Gudrun:	Nicht schneller! E-Mail kann doch schon sehr schnell geschickt werden. Aber man kann sie jetzt noch einfacher schicken.
Andreas:	Das ist ja toll. Auch unsere E-Mail Addresse ist einfach zu merken.

A New Computer

Andreas:	And what can be done better with this new computer?
Gudrun:	With the new modem one can surf the Internet faster. And one can download Web pages with graphics and video.
Andreas:	Can e-mail be sent faster, as well?
Gudrun:	Not faster! E-mail can already be sent very fast. But now it is also much easier.
Andreas:	That is terrific. Our e-mail address is easy to remember, as well.

NEW VOCABULARY

anzeigen	*to display*
beifügen	*to attach, to add*
der Browser	*Web browser*
der Computer	*computer*
die Datei	*file*
die E-Mail schicken	*to send e-mail*
die Grafik	*graphic*
herunterladen	*to download*
hochfahren	*to boot up*
das Internet surfen	*to surf the Internet*
der Mausklick	*mouse click*
das Modem	*modem*
das Netz	*Net*
der Schreibtisch	*desk*
surfen	*to surf*
toll	*terrific*
die Tonaufnahme	*audio recording*
das Video	*video*
die Webseite	*Web page*
weltweit	*worldwide*
das weltweite Netz	*World Wide Web*

LESSON 31
AUF DER BANK
At the Bank

Die Kontoeröffnung

Kunde:	Ich möchte ein neues Konto eröffnen. Ich habe schon ein Girokonto bei Ihnen. Hier ist meine Karte.
Bankangestellte:	Sie möchten ein Sparkonto einrichten?
Kunde:	Richtig. Der Zinssatz wird ja augenblicklich immer höher. Es lohnt sich.
Bankangestellte:	Ja, Sparen ist eine gut Anlage. Füllen Sie nun dieses Einzahlungsformular aus.
Kunde:	So, jetzt ist alles ausgefüllt.
Bankangestellte:	Hier ist Ihr Sparbuch.

Opening an Account

Customer:	I would like to open a new account. I already have a checking account with you. Here is my card.
Bank Employee:	Do you want to open a savings account?
Customer:	That's right. Just now the interest rate is getting higher and higher. It's worth it.
Bank Employee:	Yes, saving is a good investment. Now please fill out this deposit slip.
Customer:	Okay, everything is filled out.
Bank Employee:	Here is your passbook.

NEW VOCABULARY

abheben	*to withdraw*
die Anlage	*investment*
augenblicklich	*momentarily*
die Bank	*bank*
Es lohnt sich.	*It pays off.*
einzahlen	*to deposit*
das Einzahlungsformular	*payment slip*
erste, -r, -s	*first*
Geld umtauschen	*to exchange money*
das Girokonto	*checking account*
die Goldmünze	*gold coin*
ein Konto einrichten	*to open an account*
ein Konto eröffnen	*to open an account*
die Kontonummer	*account number*
der Kunde	*customer*
der Reisescheck	*traveler's check*
einen Scheck einlösen	*to cash a check*
das Sparbuch	*passbook*
sparen	*to save*
das Sparkonto	*savings account*
unterschreiben	*to sign*
wechseln	*to change*
die Zinsen (pl)	*interest*
der Zinssatz	*interest rate*

LESSON 32
DAS THEATER
The Theater

An der Theaterkasse

Theaterbesucherin:	Hätten Sie noch zwei Karten für die Vorstellung heute abend?
Kassierer:	Wir hätten Plätze im Parkett und im ersten Rang.
Theaterbesucherin:	Das wäre okay. Würden Sie mir bitte die Plätze auf dem Sitzplan zeigen?
Kassierer:	Hier. Parkett, dritte Reihe, rechts, fünf und sechs.
Theaterbesucherin:	Wir würden lieber links von der Bühne sitzen.
Kassierer:	Da hätte ich nur zwei Plätze hintereinander.
Theaterbesucherin:	Gut. Die nehme ich.

At the Theater Box Office

Theatergoer:	Would you still have two tickets for the performance tonight?
Cashier:	We would have seats in the orchestra and in the dress circle.
Theatergoer:	That would be okay. Would you please show me the seats on the seating plan?
Cashier:	Here. Orchestra, third row, on the right side, five and six.
Theatergoer:	We would prefer to sit on the left of the stage.
Cashier:	There we'd only have two seats, one behind the other.
Theatergoer:	Alright. I'll take them.

NEW VOCABULARY

die Bühne	*stage*
dritte Reihe	*third row*
hätten	*would have*
helfen	*to help*
hintereinander	*behind one another*
im ersten Rang	*in the dress circle*
im Parkett	*in the orchestra*
klatschen	*to applaud*
lachen	*to laugh*
leise	*quiet, calm*
das Kino	*movie theater*
die Pause	*intermission*
der Platz	*seat*
Rauchen verboten!	*No smoking!*
der Schauspieler	*actor*
der Sitzplan	*seating plan*
das Taschentuch	*handkerchief*
das Theater	*theater*
die Vorstellung	*performance*
wären	*would be*
würden	*would*

LESSON 33
FESTE
Festivals

Karneval/Fasching

Andreas: Nina würde uns ihre Karten für den
          Maskenball am Rosenmontag schenken.
          Hättest du Lust mitzukommen?

Dorothee: Und ob! Also ob ich nicht immer dafür zu
          haben wäre. Aber wie verkleiden wir uns?

Andreas: Nina meinte, ich hätte großen Erfolg, wenn
          ich als Unsichtbarer gehen würde.

Dorothee: Oh, wenn ich dich den ganzen Abend nicht
          sehen würde, hätte Dornröschen doch
          keinen Prinzen.

Andreas: Macht ja nichts. Als Dornröschen würdest du
          doch sowieso nur schlafen.

Carnival

Andreas: *Nina would give us her tickets for the ball
          on Rose Monday. Do you feel like coming
          along?*

Dorothee: *You bet! As if I wasn't always up to it. But
          how do we dress up?*

Andreas: *Nina said I'd have a lot of success if I went
          as the invisible man.*

Dorothee: *Oh, if I didn't see you all evening, Sleeping
          Beauty wouldn't have a prince.*

Andreas: *Doesn't matter. As Sleeping Beauty you'd
          sleep anyway.*

NEW VOCABULARY

als ob	*as if*
das Dornröschen	*Sleeping Beauty*
der Erfolg	*success*
feiern	*to celebrate*
das Fest	*party*
Ich bin dafür zu haben.	*I'm all for it.*
der Kater	*hangover*
der Maskenball	*costume ball*
mitmachen	*to join the action*
Prost!	*Cheers!*
der Rosenmontag	*Rose Monday (festival)*
sich verkleiden	*to masquerade, to disguise*
sowieso	*anyway*
der Umzug	*parade*
Und ob!	*You bet!*
unsichtbar	*invisible*
Zum Wohl!	*To your health!*

LESSON 34
DIE MEDIEN
The Media

Information ist Alles

Elisabeth:	Rudy, wir sind gar nicht auf dem Laufenden. Der Fernseher geht nicht, und die Zeitung kommt schon seit zwei Tagen nicht.
Rudy:	Aber warum kommt denn die Zeitung nicht?
Elisabeth:	Ich glaube, der Zeitungsjunge ist krank.
Rudy:	Und wann wird die Antenne für unseren neuen Fernseher installiert?
Elisabeth:	Ich habe keine Ahnung. Sie haben gar nichts darüber gesagt.
Rudy:	Dann müssen wir eben die Nachrichten im Radio hören.
Elisabeth:	Aber wir haben doch gar kein Radio mehr.
Rudy:	Das darf doch nicht wahr sein.

Information is Everything

Elisabeth:	Rudy, we're not up-to-date at all. The TV doesn't work, and the newspaper didn't come for two days.
Rudy:	But why does the newspaper not come?
Elisabeth:	I believe the paperboy is sick.
Rudy:	And when is the antenna for our new TV set being installed?
Elisabeth:	I don't have any idea. They didn't mention anything about that at all.
Rudy:	Then we'll just have to listen to the news on the radio.
Elisabeth:	But we don't have a radio anymore.
Rudy:	I really can't believe that.

NEW VOCABULARY

die Ahnung	*idea, clue*
die Antenne	*antenna*
auf dem Laufenden sein	*to be up-to-date*
blass	*faint, pale*
doch	*really, indeed*
eben	*just*
Es geht nicht.	*It doesn't work.*
der Fernseher	*TV set*
die Fernsehsendung	*TV show*
gar	*fully, very, quite*
Ich habe keine Ahnung.	*I have no idea.*
der Moderator	*anchorman*
die Nachricht	*news*
die Nachrichten (pl)	*news*
der Nachrichtensprecher	*news anchor*
wahr	*true*
der Wetterbericht	*weather report*
die Zeitung	*newspaper*
der Zeitungsjunge	*paperboy*

LESSON 35
MUSEEN
Museums

Im Museum

Karin: Wie gefällt dir diese Austellung?

Sarah: Die meisten Gemälde und Plastiken finde ich ein wenig seltsam.

Karin: Möchtest du noch einen anderen Raum anschauen?

Sarah: Wie wär's mit der Malerei des Mittelalters?

Karin: Gibt es nicht eine Sonderausstellung über moderne Töpferei und Glas?

Sarah: Gute Idee. Und die ist nur noch drei Tage geöffnet.

At the Museum

Karin: How do you like this exhibition?

Sarah: I find most of the pictures and sculptures a bit strange.

Karin: Would you like to look at another room?

Sarah: How about medieval paintings?

Karin: Isn't there a special exhibit of modern pottery and glass?

Sarah: Good idea. And it's only going to be there for another three days.

NEW VOCABULARY

die Ausstellung	*exhibition*
der Bildhauer	*sculptor*
Das hört sich gut an!	*Sounds good!*
gefallen	*to like*
gern haben	*to like*
das Gemälde	*painting*
die Kunst	*art*
der Künstler	*artist*
lieben	*to love*
die Malerei	*painting*
das Mittelalter	*Middle Ages*
die Plastik	*sculpture*
der Raum	*room*
seltsam	*awkward*
die Sonderausstellung	*special exhibition*
die Töpferei	*pottery*
die Zeichnung	*drawing*

GRAMMAR SUMMARY

1. The Definite Article

	MASCULINE	FEMININE	NEUTER	PLURAL
NOMINATIVE	der	die	das	die
ACCUSATIVE	den	die	das	die
DATIVE	dem	der	dem	den
GENITIVE	des	der	des	der

2. der-Words: *dieser, jener, welcher, manche, solche*

	MASCULINE	FEMININE	NEUTER	PLURAL
NOMINATIVE	dieser	diese	dieses	diese
ACCUSATIVE	diesen	diese	dieses	diese
DATIVE	diesem	dieser	diesem	diesen
GENITIVE	dieses	dieser	dieses	dieser

3. The Indefinite Article

	MASCULINE	FEMININE	NEUTER
NOMINATIVE	ein	eine	ein
ACCUSATIVE	einen	eine	ein
DATIVE	einem	einer	einem
GENITIVE	eines	einer	eines

4. ein-Words: *kein, mein, dein, sein, ihr, unser, euer, ihr, Ihr*

	MASCULINE	FEMININE	NEUTER	PLURAL
NOMINATIVE	mein	meine	mein	meine
ACCUSATIVE	meinen	meine	mein	meine
DATIVE	meinem	meiner	meinem	meinen
GENITIVE	meines	meiner	meines	meiner

5. Masculine n-Nouns

	SINGULAR	PLURAL
NOMINATIVE	der Architekt	die Architekten
ACCUSATIVE	den Architekten	die Architekten
DATIVE	dem Architekten	den Architekten
GENITIVE	des Architekten	der Architekten

Other masculine n-nouns include:

der Bauer	der Fotograf	der Nachbar
der Bursche	der Journalist	der Präsident
der Diplomat	der Jurist	der Zeuge
der Experte	der Mensch	

6. Preceded Adjectives

	MASCULINE	FEMININE	NEUTER
NOMINATIVE	der junge Mann	die alte Stadt	das schöne Haus
	ein junger Mann	eine alte Stadt	ein schönes Haus
ACCUSATIVE	den jungen Mann	die alte Stadt	das schöne Haus
	einen jungen Mann	eine alte Stadt	ein schönes Haus
DATIVE	dem jungen Mann	der alten Stadt	dem schönen Haus
	einem jungen Mann	einer alten Stadt	einem schönen Haus
GENITIVE	des jungen Mannes	der alten Stadt	des schönen Hauses
	eines jungen Mannes	einer alten Stadt	eines schönen Hause

	PLURAL
NOMINATIVE	die guten Weine
	keine guten Weine
ACCUSATIVE	die guten Weine
	keine guten Weine
DATIVE	den guten Weinen
	keinen guten Weines
GENITIVE	der guten Weine
	keiner guten Weines

7. Unpreceded Adjectives

	MASCULINE	FEMININE	NEUTER
NOMINATIVE	guter Kuchen	gute Torte	gutes Brot
ACCUSATIVE	guten Kuchen	gute Torte	gutes Brot
DATIVE	gutem Kuchen	guter Torte	gutem Brot
GENITIVE	guten Kuchens	guter Torte	guten Brotes

	PLURAL
NOMINATIVE	gute Torten
ACCUSATIVE	gute Torten
DATIVE	guten Torten
GENITIVE	guter Torten

8. Personal Pronouns

SINGULAR	1ST PERSON	2ND PERSON	3RD PERSON MASCULINE	3RD PERSON FEMININE	3RD PERSON NEUTER
NOMINATIVE	ich	du	er	sie	es
ACCUSATIVE	mich	dich	ihn	sie	es
DATIVE	mir	dir	ihm	ihr	ihm

PLURAL	1ST PERSON	2ND PERSON	3RD PERSON	POLITE
NOMINATIVE	wir	ihr	sie	Sie
ACCUSATIVE	uns	euch	sie	Sie
DATIVE	uns	euch	ihnen	Ihnen

9. Question Words

warum?	*why?*
wieviel?	*how much?*
weshalb?	*why?*
wer?	*who?*
weswegen?	*why?*
wie?	*how?*
wieso?	*why?*
wozu?	*what for?*
wann?	*when?*
was?	*what?*
wo?	*where?*

10. Forms of *wer* and *was*

NOMINATIVE	wer?	was?
ACCUSATIVE	wen?	was?
DATIVE	wem?	
GENITIVE	wessen?	

11. The Demonstrative Pronoun *der*

	MASCULINE	FEMININE	NEUTER	PLURAL
NOMINATIVE	der	die	das	die
ACCUSATIVE	den	die	das	die
DATIVE	dem	der	dem	denen

12. Relative Pronouns

	MASCULINE	FEMININE	NEUTER	PLURAL
NOMINATIVE	der	die	das	die
ACCUSATIVE	den	die	das	die
DATIVE	dem	der	dem	denen
GENITIVE	dessen	deren	dessen	deren

13. Reflexive Pronouns

	SINGULAR	PLURAL
1ST PERSON	mich	uns
2ND PERSON	dich	euch
3RD PERSON	sich	sich

14. Comparative and Superlative

POSITIVE	COMPARATIVE	SUPERLATIVE (ADJ.)	SUPERLATIVE (ADV.)
gut	besser	beste, -r, -s	am besten
groß	größer	größte, -r, -s	am größten
hoch	höher	höchste, -r, -s	am höchsten
nahe	näher	nächste, -r, -s	am nächsten
viel	mehr	meiste, -r, -s	am meisten
gern	lieber	liebste, -r, -s	am liebsten

15. Verbs in the Indicative

PRESENT

I ask, I am asking, I do ask

ich	frage
du	fragst
er/sie/es	fragt
wir	fragen
ihr	fragt
sie	fragen
Sie	fragen

PRESENT PERFECT

I have asked, I asked, I did ask

ich	habe gefragt
du	hast gefragt
er/sie/es	hat gefragt
wir	haben gefragt
ihr	habt gefragt
sie	haben gefragt
Sie	haben gefragt

I have come, I came, I did come

ich	bin gekommen
du	bist gekommen
er/sie/es	ist gekommen
wir	sind gekommen
ihr	seid gekommen
sie	sind gekommen
Sie	sind gekommen

SIMPLE PAST

I asked, I was asking

ich	fragte
du	fragtest
er/sie/es	fragte
wir	fragten
ihr	fragtet
sie	fragten
Sie	fragten

I came, I was coming

ich	kam
du	kamst
er/sie/es	kam
wir	kamen
ihr	kamt
sie	kamen
Sie	kamen

PAST PERFECT

I had asked

ich	hatte gefragt
du	hattest gefragt
er/sie/es	hatte gefragt
wir	hatten gefragt
ihr	hattet gefragt
sie	hatten gefragt
Sie	hatten gefragt

I had come

ich	war gekommen
du	warst gekommen
er/sie/es	war gekommen
wir	waren gekommen
ihr	wart gekommen
sie	waren gekommen
Sie	waren gekommen

FUTURE

I will ask

ich	werde fragen
du	wirst fragen
er/sie/es	wird fragen
wir	werden fragen
ihr	werdet fragen
sie	werden fragen
Sie	werden fragen

GLOSSARY OF GRAMMATICAL TERMS

active voice—das Aktiv: *a verb form in which the subject of the verb is active, i.e., performs an action.*

adjective—das Adjektiv: *a word that describes nouns, as for example* hübsch (*pretty*).

adverb—das Adverb: *a word that describes verbs, adjectives, or other adverbs, as for example* schnell (*quickly*).

auxiliary verb—das Hilfsverb: *a helping verb used with a main verb to form compound tenses. German has three:* haben (*to have*), sein (*to be*), *and* werden (*to become*).

compound tense—die zusammengesetzte Zeit: *a tense formed with one of the auxiliaries* haben, sein, *or* werden, *such as the conversational past or the future.*

conditional—das Konditional: *the mood used for hypothetical (depending on a possible condition or circumstance) statements and questions.*

conjugation—die Konjugation: *the system of verb forms with their endings that express tense, person, and number.*

conversational past—das Perfekt: *a verb form used to express actions or states that happened in the past; used mainly in conversation.*

definite article—der bestimmte Artikel: *a word linked to a noun indicating it is specific, as for example* der (*the*).

demonstrative—das Demonstrativpronomen und -adjektiv: *words that highlight something that is referred to, as for example* dieses Buch (*this book*).

der-words—der-Wörter: *words that are conjugated exactly like the definite article, such as* dieser (*this*).

ein-words—ein-Wörter: *words that are conjugated exactly like the indefinite article, such as kein (none).*

ending—die Endung: *the suffixes added to the stem, indicating person, tense, and mood.*

gender—das Geschlecht: *grammatical categories for nouns, loosely related to physical gender and/or word ending; German has three—masculine, feminine, and neuter: der Mann (m), die Frau (f), das Kind (n).*

imperative—Imperativ: *the command form.*

impersonal verb—das unpersönliche Verb: *a group of verbs usually only used with an impersonal subject such as es (it) or das (that). For example: Es regnet (It's raining).*

indefinite article—der unbestimmte Artikel: *a word linked to a noun indicating that it is nonspecific, as for example: ein (a/an).*

indicative—der Indikativ: *the mood used for factual or objective statements and questions.*

infinitive—der Infinitiv: *the basic form of a verb found in the dictionary that does not specify the subject (person or number), tense, or mood. The German infinitive always ends in -en. For example: sprechen (to speak).*

inseparable verb—das untrennbare Verb: *verbs with a prefix that cannot be separated from the verb. For example: bekommen (to get).*

intransitive verb—intransitives Verb: *a verb denoting a complete action without taking a direct object, such as sitzen (to sit).*

irregular verb—das unregelmäßige Verb: *a group of verbs that undergo a stem-vowel change in their narrative past, and sometimes even in some forms of the present indicative. For example: ich verstehe—ich verstand. See also "strong verb."*

mixed verb—das gemischte Verb: *a group of verbs that form their narrative past and their past participle with a vowel change (like strong verbs)* *and the weak verb endings. For example: brennen—brannte—gebrannt. See also "semi-regular verb."*

modal verb—das Modalverb: *a group of six irregular verbs expressing permission, ability, wish, obligation, and necessity: dürfen, können, wollen, möchten, sollen, müssen.*

mood—der Modus: *the attitude toward what is expressed by the verb. See also "indicative," "conditional," and "subjunctive."*

narrative past—die einfache Vergangenheit: *the past tense used for completed actions or states; useful for narration of events.*

noun—der Substantiv: *a word referring to a person, place, or thing, as for example das Haus (house).*

number—die Zahl: *the distinction between singular and plural.*

object—das Objekt: *a grammatical object can be a noun, pronoun, or noun group governed by a transitive verb or a preposition. It may be a direct object, i.e., the person or thing that receives the action of a verb (Akkusativ—accusative), or an indirect object, i.e., the person or thing that receives the action of the direct object and/or is the object of a preposition (Dativ—dative).*

participle—das Partizip: *an unconjugated, unchanging verb form often used with auxiliary verbs to form compound verb forms. For example: present and past participles: essend/gegessen (eating/eaten).*

passive voice—das Passiv: *a verb form in which the recipient of the action is expressed as the grammatical subject.*

past perfect—das Plusquamperfekt: *the past perfect using the narrative past of haben (to have) or sein (to be) plus the past participle.*

perfect—das Perfekt: *verb forms used for actions or states that are already completed.*

person—die Person: *the grammatical category that distinguishes between the speaker (first person), the person spoken to (second person), and the* people and things spoken about (third person); often applies to pronouns and verbs.

possessive pronoun—das Possessivpronomen: *indicates ownership, as for example* mein (*me*).

predictable verb—das regelmäßige Verb: *a group of regular verbs that form their narrative past by adding endings to their stem, as for example* holen—holte. *Their past participle always adds the prefix* ge- *and the ending* -t: holen—geholt. *See also "weak verb."*

preposition—die Präposition: *a word (often as part of a phrase) that expresses spatial, temporal, and other relationships, as for example* auf (*on*).

present—das Präsens: *verb forms used for actions or states that are in progress.*

pronoun—das Pronomen: *a word taking the place of a noun, as for example personal or demonstrative pronouns.*

reflexive verb—das reflexive Verb: *a verb whose action reflects back to the subject, as for example* sich baden (*to bathe oneself*).

semi-regular verb—das semi-regelmäßige Verb: *a group of verbs that form the narrative past and the past participle with a stem-vowel change (like strong verbs) and the weak verb endings. For example:* brennen—brannte—gebrannt. *See also "mixed verb."*

separable verb—das trennbare Verb: *verbs with a prefix that is separated from the verb in certain tenses and moods. For example:* ankommen (*to arrive*); Ich komme an (*I'm arriving*).

simple tense—die nichtzusammengesetzte Zeit: *a tense such as the narrative past that is formed by adding endings to the verb stem.*

stem or root—der Stamm: *the basic part of the infinitive that does not change during the conjugation of regular verbs formed by dropping the* -en *ending.*

strong verb—das starke Verb: *a group of verbs that form the narrative past and sometimes their past participle with a vowel change, as for example* singen—sang—gesungen. *Their past participle always ends in* -en.

subject—das Subjekt: *the person, place, or thing performing the action of the verb or being in the state described by it* (nominative).

subjunctive—der Konjunktiv: *the mood used for nonfactual or subjective statements or questions.*

tense—die Zeit: *the time of an action or state, i.e., past, present, future.*

transitive verb—das transitive Verb: *a verb denoting a complete action accompanied by a direct object, such as* setzen (to put).

verb—das Verb: *a word expressing an action or state, as for example* gehen (to walk).

weak verb—das schwache Verb: *a group of verbs that form their narrative past by adding endings to their stem, as for example* holen—holte. *Their past participle always adds the prefix* ge- *and the ending* -t: holen—geholt. *See also "predictable verb."*